Flux

Wilms

BookLeaf Publishing

India | USA | UK

Made with ❤ on the BookLeaf Publishing Platform
www.bookleafpub.in
www.bookleafpub.com

Dedication

for the people who feel stuck,
for the ones at their lowest,
for those standing on a ledge,
don't give up now, don't stop going,
because i promise, it gets better.

Preface

Change is hard. Anyone who says otherwise is lying to you. Sure, there are people who deal with it better than others, but that doesn't change the fact that it's still hard. Attending college when you're at the cusp of adulthood and experiencing the most physiological growth your body will ever face is arguably the single most impactful change a teenager goes through.

Flux is a novice attempt by an experienced individual to express what we all go through as we start a new part of life, embarking on the journey where we truly discover ourselves as individuals separate from our family, trying to carve out our own identity, learning along the way and growing more independent each day. From falling in love to falling out of it, from new experiences to terrible lows, the contents of this book aim to strike a chord with how we felt at our absolute worst - the sorrow and the loneliness and the pain in our hearts - and how we got ourselves up and dusted ourselves off and lived to give our best another day, because that is the most difficult choice we make everyday despite what we face and endure.

I wrote these more or less in succession, with the

anthology ending on a higher note than most of the poems that are part of it, but everyone might not feel them in that same order. However, that shouldn't stop every single person out there to resonate with these writings one way or another, and think back on those instances that felt so life-defining when they happened but seem like fleeting memories now, stars charged with emotion in the sky that is the story of our life.

Acknowledgements

Appreciating the people working at BookLeaf Publishing is a must for making this process as easy and smooth as it could have possibly been, and for helping my dreams come true.

I'd also like to thank my parents. Even though they don't know it yet, it's their money that made this book possible. Hopefully, I make them and my younger brother proud with it. I'm grateful for my friends for being there to help me out not just while this book was in the works, but for when I was going through everything these lines talk about and more. I couldn't have made it this far enough without them pushing me through it all.

Finally, I sincerely thank every single person who takes the time out to read this book, hoping they always remember that they aren't alone, and that there are millions of people in the world who are going through something similar, maybe even feeling the same. It's like Ranata Suzuki said: "at least we are under the same sky".

1. Spiral

It's all a spiral.
I can't walk out of it.
I keep going,
But it never ends.
A wave washes over me,
I can't stay afloat.
The thoughts surround me,
They're not my own,
But they control me now.
The storm rages on.
I keep trying to reach its eye,
But i can't see my path ahead.
It's all a spiral,
And i can't walk out of it.

2. Stop

this is all just so much
i can't take it anymore
i need my escape
the walls are closing in
everyone and everything surrounds me
I'm losing myself
I'm disappearing

3. Hope

There are so many colours here and so much noise
It's not easy to keep my head straight and my mind clear
My only hope is the one
The one who carries me to the light
And helps me find myself
And believes in me more than I ever could
It is almost poetic that she is bound to leave me
I do not possess the quality to go on without her
Now that i know what it is like to be in her arms
I will never be able to show her these words
Never be able to tell her what she means to me
She is not my love, love is an earthly concept
And she is from the heavens
I can only wish to find her again
In this life, and the next

4. I See Her

I see her.
I see her as clearly as the seas and the stars.
I see her laugh.
I see the smile in her eyes when she sees me.
I see her crying when I pull away.
I see myself sinking deeper.
I see an unfathomable chasm.
I see the ocean of thoughts in her mind,
Crashing against the doors of my heart,
Calling me to dive in them,
And drown myself in its dreams.
I see her coming out of the darkness,
And leading me into the light.
I see a house,
With someone who looks just like me,
Lying in his cradle, and crying in her arms.
I see her still, like the sun on a rainy day,
Always there for me,
Even when I don't see her.

5. Something Funny For Her

She asked me to write something funny for her
She doesn't know I'm already dying to make her smile
Every time I get too flirty with her,
She threatens me with 'maar
I'm so used to being the funny one,
I'm confused about the way she makes me laugh
Maybe I shouldn't be doing this with a fortnight left in
the same state?
I HATE LIFE FOR THROWING SUCH A PERFECT GIRL
MY WAY

6. Free

You were never for me,
You were a dream faraway,
Something for me to see and adore,
But never to receive.
Now that I know this,
I can relish what we had,
I can recall your face,
Beautiful as the cherry blossoms in spring,
And be grateful for having enjoyed your company for as
long as I did.
I'm happy that I've finally let go of you,
I'm happy that I've finally set myself free.

7. Left

I gave you my all
When we were together,
Now you're gone,
And I have nothing left in me.
Maybe I shouldn't have,
But I don't know how to love halfway.
Now I don't love at all,
Because I have nothing left in me.

8. Better

we spoke about what it would be like to be together
today
it felt so good at first, but then i remembered
it was all just a sweet dream
we aren't gonna be together,
but GOD it was nice to imagine,
awaking to her call everyday,
sleeping to her i love you's
who knows, maybe one day she'll fall for me too,
maybe one day i'll be more to her
but until then, i'll pack my dreams in a bag
and take them with me
till i lose them to my past,
or a better reality

9. Urge

Fighting the urge to take her face in my hands,
To pull her in and hold her close to me forever,
To kiss her on the head and watch her go to sleep every night,
To follow her around with a flower in my hand for her everyday,
To ask her to give me a chance to make her mine

10. In A Novel

My best friend thinks she's gorgeous and has the
prettiest smile - I don't agree
No words will ever be enough to describe her
Shakespeare could fall short of praises to sing about her
beauty,
And Neruda's verses would not do justice to her heart
She seems more like the protagonist of a John Green
novel,
Impeccable, inexplicable, and surreal
She could be right there and still be out of reach for me
I just hope there's less of the latter in our bittersweet
ending

11. Burn

she said she wasn't sure
she said she was confused
but now she isn't
there can't be smoke without fire
right?
wrong
she said there's no spark
but she managed to burn my love like a cigarette
funny that she doesn't even drag
but every time she becomes a sponge
my demons come out again
i fight to keep them inside
but i don't know how much longer i can face them,
how much longer i can face her

12. Half

you were looking for love
i gave my heart to you, and you threw it away
now you're unloved, and i'm heartless

i'm ready to follow you into the deepest and darkest
abyss
but you're looking for tenderness, warmth and intimacy
in temples of lust
that's not something i can see you do,
hurt yourself because it's what you're used to

13. Not There

even when we're there, we're not
she is, and i am, but we're not
we're lying in the same bed
but we're not lying together
i miss how we used to sleep,
holding each other without a thought
until the morning sun made her skin sparkle golden
it feels like Ed Sheeran wrote Afterglow with her face in
his mind

14. Longer

i'm trying my best to be okay,
i'm trying so hard to keep a smile
there's no way to know how long,
just how long i can continue this facade,
how long i can go on without a word
to the people i so desperately need to say it to,
how much longer i can wait for them to understand,
just by seeing the pain in my eyes
that there's no way i can keep going like this

15. Sunk

*I'm not sure if I'm moving on
it looks like i am?
but there's this inherent heaviness that's weighing me
down,
like my heart knows that all attempts to replace her are
futile
seeing her doesn't hurt as much as before,
but i think of her now, more than i ever did
the acceptance has sunk inside me,
and my soul with it,
pulling and dragging me down inside my own head
until there's nothing but one thought washing over me-
the image of her sunkissed face smiling down at me,
wondering if I'll ever kiss her
i wish I'd kissed her*

16. Can't

i just sat there, staring at my phone
wondering what I'd done to deserve this,
the insults and the hate
that were just stemming from lies
or were they right?
was i in the wrong?
am i really that bad?
i don't think i am
i would like to think that I'm not
but I'm not so sure,
not anymore

17. Lost

i thought it would help,
to not see
her perfect face as much,
to not hold her
like we were going to spend eternity in each other's arms
i thought it would help to stay away,
to not hear her voice,
to not let her name roll off my tongue,
to not wait to see her materialize when i open the door
i was so wrong
the guilt of seeing her hurt from a distance
weighs me down like the world on atlas
why do i ache on seeing her pain
as if her actions were not aching me enough?

18. Past

every time i see a face from my past,
the nightmares come running back
doesn't matter if they lasted for an hour, a week, a
month, or a year
they'll haunt me for the rest of my life
the words don't go away,
no matter how much i try to bury them in the depths of
my mind,
they keep pulling me down,
making me sink with them, not letting me leave them
behind

19. Pieces Of Me//A New Muse?

i gave her pieces of me,
so she wouldn't be broken anymore
she took the pieces and gave them to someone else
i showed her parts of my mind
nobody would want to take home
she didn't, either
i thought she understood me better than anybody else,
i was right
she went and hit me where it hurt the most anyway
now there's pieces of me
scattered across the ground
and nobody to help me pick them up

i found my muse,
then i lost her
even after all this time
i still look for her
her memories haunt me
because they can't complete
every girl i see

20. Bad Thing

every time i do nothing,
my mind spirals about everything
is it my fault that i always give my all until i don't,
that i either go all the way or i don't?
should i learn to hold back a little,
even when i don't want to,
for the sake of my weary heart?
is it better to love a little and stop
than to lose all the love i have,
and add to the bittersweet memories?
is it a bad thing that i sometimes go so numb
i can't even will myself to feel something
for someone so great?
is it the fault of those who stepped on me,
or mine for giving them something to step on?

21. Numb

how do you feel so much pain, that you stop feeling at
all?
how do you eventually just go so numb that nothing
affects you anymore?
people can't push you if you already jumped off the cliff
words can't act like stones if your glass walls shattered a
long time ago
you can't take things with a pinch of salt if you're
starving
you can't feel the hurt you receive if you give away your
whole heart to someone who loses it

i could let go of this pain with a breath,
i could push her away and feel nothing at all
but it won't feel right to force the throbbing storm inside
me,
and it won't feel right to open pandora's box and let the
winds out either
my feelings for her need to end naturally,
so i can still look her in the eye and tell her i waited,
tell myself i did no wrong,
and convince myself that she wasn't the right one

22. Lonely

it all feels so empty
so damn lonely
i like talking to all of them
but at the same time
i don't want to talk to all of them
i want one
to be there for
and who'll be there with me
someone who i can go to
at anytime
and know she'll be there
is it too much to ask for,
some stability in my life?

23. The Chase

is it smart to chase something with someone who doesn't
believe in what you're chasing so passionately?
am i being oblivious to the most obvious thing?
is it a dumb decision to make,
is she someone else's risk to take?
am i just hurting myself all over again,
but this time i know what i'm doing, and i'm doing it
anyway?
maybe i'm just overthinking this
maybe like every other time,
i should just do my best and see where it leads

24. A New Love

it's sweet,

that feeling when i meet someone

and i just know that that person is going to be special to

me

i know that she's going to mean something to me

i see the same spark in her eyes that i can feel in my own

i see the smile at the edge of her lips as she sees me

seeing her

the intimacy of a shared glance,

that eye contact before someone pulls away,

the tension that's so sharp you could play perfect on it

like a guitar string,

all of this leading to my hands on the back of her neck,

her fingers in my hair,

until finally

i get to kiss her lips,

her body lightly brushing against mine until i pull her

closer in,

the rush of red on her face when i finally pull back,

her face lighting up with a laugh that could bring peace

to our world,

as i clasp the soft skin on her palms in mine,

walking into the unknown with nothing but us on our

minds

25. Kiss

i really wanna kiss her
i'm scared of ruining what we have
her lips are so appealing
i wish i wasn't so insecure about people liking me
i would honestly not mind staring at those for the rest of
eternity
what if it's never the same again?
but what fun would it be to never be able to feel them
is it too much of a risk to take over our friendship?
i hope i'll get to know what she tastes like

26. No Ending//Here

i love her with every essence of my heart, mind and soul
even when i should not, i still love her

i've already lost parts of her that were never really mine,
to someone who was never really hers
i'm not sure if keeping her around is worth it still,
after all the tornadoes of spiraling thoughts in my head

i want to talk to her
she's sitting right in front of me
but i can't
the guilt will bear upon me too much
i don't want to hurt her
no matter how much it hurts me

27. The War//Lately

28. Me, Always

why is it that i always end up
falling in love with the wrong girl?
am i not as good of a judge of character as i think,
or is it just my bad luck?
are they really never in the right space,
or is it just a fault in me?
do i really always catch them at a bad time,
acting like the cushion to their broken dreams,
or is there just something fundamentally romantically
unlikeable in me?
how is it possible that it's always them, never me?
how am i "such a great guy",
but i still never get the girl i like?

29. A Little Empty

everything seems lesser now
from my enthusiasm for life,
to the joy i find in spending time with my friends
it all seems like a distant memory
that's slowly losing its colour,
slowly but surely turning grey
nothing seems significant,
nothing makes life worthwhile

except for those little moments i have with her
which, despite her not reciprocating my affection,
seem like the best part of my day
like I'd move heaven and earth for them,
like I'd walk over the mountains and swim the seas,
all to see her smile at the end of it

30. Much

how much is too much?
when do you stop without feeling the guilt of stopping?
how deep can you sink to save someone without
drowning in the sea too?
how far do you stretch your hand to save someone else
before falling as well?
at what point do you stop looking for someone else
before losing yourself too?
when is it okay to take a breath and tell yourself that you
gave it your all?

31. Down

everything in me, i put out there
but instead of holding it,
you let it go,
you let it fall to the floor
instead of helping me back up,
you left my broken pieces down there,
all alone
and now i can't move on
because i don't have enough left of me
to go forth

32. Think I Am

i don't think I'm as great as i think i am,
as great as i thought i was
i try to pretend that I'm okay about it,
but I'm really not
i try my best to get better,
to be better,
but i don't think it's helping
hopefully, one day, it does

33. Broken

broken boy, broken strings
can't play perfect anymore
Icarus with my chipped wings,
falling down on all four

34. Decision

i can't give away anymore of me,
if i don't have anything in me to give
when will i accept that there's nothing
i could've said or done to change her mind,
it was her choice to make, after all,
the decision was never mine

35. Flux

i'm in medias res
i'm still in a flux
idk if i should stop and start again
idk if i have the strength to go on
i need to get better
i need to do better
i'll die, before
i give in to the thoughts in my mind

36. Relive

i did not know heaven existed,
until that lazy afternoon
when we just held each other,
and you fell asleep in my arms
i wish i could play that back
and relive that time,
i wish i could kiss you on the head
and look in your eyes
and stare at your smile
for the rest of my life

37. Funny//Interesting

it was right there, bright and clear,
in front of my face, in front of my eyes,
but they refused to see it,
my mind refused to acknowledge the truth
how was i supposed to believe
that there was not enough for her to hold,
even after all this time?
i wish my mind was like a blank piece of paper,
her memories wiped clean and erased
as soon as they got too heavy for me to carry

38. Move

how do i choose
if every choice is wrong??
how can i choose
if noone wants to be my choice?
how is it wrong for me to move quick
if everyone moves away and nobody stays?
everyone calls me emotionless, but they don't know
I'm really just hiding my emotions
because i have too many, i feel too much,
more than they can take

39. Stay

can you stay the night,
spend your time on me?
take care of my heart,
set me free
I'll bring you the moon
if it lights up the stars in your eyes,
I'll burn the world if you shed a tear,
who cares if that's my vice

40. Enough

Where do you go when you're lying in your bed?
How do you cope when we're not together?
How do you feel about us not being together?
Everytime these thoughts run around my mind,
I lose myself a little more.
Maybe we're meant to be, maybe we're not,
Maybe we just need to see,
This is what we've been chasing all our lives,
And now that we have it,
We shouldn't let go.
Maybe we just need to stop and breathe,
Maybe we just need to stay in this moment,
'cause all I wanna do is hold onto you,
And never let you go.
Maybe that's all we need,
Maybe that's enough.

www.ingramcontent.com/pod-product-compliance
Lightning Source LLC
La Vergne TN
LVHW021306200726
843509LV00012B/1808